NEW KID DICTIONARY

NEW KID
DICTIONARY

edited by LAZAR SARNA

Adelaide Books
New York / Lisbon
2021

NEW KID DICTIONARY
By Lazar Sarna

Copyright © by Lazar Sarna
Cover design © 2021 Adelaide Books

Published by Adelaide Books, New York / Lisbon
adelaidebooks.org
Editor-in-Chief
Stevan V. Nikolic

For any information, please address Adelaide Books
at info@adelaidebooks.org
or write to:
Adelaide Books
244 Fifth Ave. Suite D27
New York, NY, 10001

ISBN: 978-1-955196-97-0

Printed in the United States of America

To my Jewel,

whose perception of life matches mine

Contents

INTRODUCTION

The New Kid Dictionary is a compilation of original expressions, queries, explanations and utterances, (all off-the-cuff) by kids and adults faced with usually common or surprising circumstances. These have been captured and set down here in their original form, thereby preserving the humour, innocence, joy and curiosity that language can offer.

Sometimes the wording may be twisted or incomplete. Often the idea is there but half-baked in its expression. These sayings capture a stage in life and a snap-shot of a moment frozen forever in this book.

The contents are not meant to make fun of anyone: on the contrary they glorify the creativity and courage of expression. They summarize in a way the path travelled by two of the Offers (Authors) during their fifty years of marriage.

PART ONE:
CONVERSATIONS

A

ANIMALS

He barks every morning at 6 o'clock.

He thinks he's a rooster.

Jewel, describing the neighbour's dog.

I like dogs.....with no teeth.

Uncle Aaron,
lamenting the rarity of such canines.

Horse-fish.

Tova, trying to translate
the Hebrew word for sea-horse.

ANOMALIES

I'm hot. I need earmuffs made of ice.

Ice muffs.

> *Dov, reacting to the temperature.*

This marshmallow is good even after Tat stepped on it.

> *Michi, savouring a surprisingly good snack.*

If no-one wants the gefilte fish juice, I'm going to drink all of it myself.

> *Jewel, never wanting to let good food go to waste.*

Everyone has a cell phone. Why can't I have one?

Tat doesn't have one.

......(Quizzical silence)

> *Eitan, trying to convince his mother.*

ANSWERING MACHINE

I'm only accepting messages from wrong numbers.

Please leave a message before the beep.

Hello, I'm not here, I'm elsewhere. Where else?

Please leave a message unless you're uni-neuronal.

Please leave a message in sign language or Morse-code.

Please leave a message if you're carbon-based.

Please leave a message while yodeling.

Please leave a message in hieroglyphics.

Hi, this is the guy you're calling. Please leave a message.

Dov's recorded messages
on his answering machine.

ATMOSPHERE

It's still light outside. I'm going to sleep wrong.

Racheli, negotiating with her parents
to let her stay up later.

Why does my car always smell like a falafel stand?

Tova, taking a deep breath.

It looks like the emergency ward at the hospital.

Jewel, walking into a crowded restaurant

-Why do you close the door?

-I want my primacy.

Ezra, talking bathroom etiquette with Avi.

Don't go there. You'll come back pregnant.

Marie-Josee Weigensberg
recalling her trip to Israel.

Tat's bathroom smells like strawberries.

Hillel's observation.

B

BEAUTY

Don't eat near my head. I'm going to sell my hair.

Teenage Naomi.

I'm getting to the age when my legs feel old.

Adult Naomi chasing her kids.

Do you have a neck?

Ella Weigensberg, looking at people's heads.

There's no such thing as Flemish.

*Michi, upon hearing what
they speak in Belgium.*

You are the cutest girl I ever met-ted.

Daveed to Racheli.

My beard felt like a living pet on my face.

Jessy, after shaving his summer growth.

I don't like your shirt. I don't like your skirt.....and I
don't like your skin.

Nava, sizing up Jewel's attire.

It's a work of art. We don't poke a hole in it with
our finger.

Naomi to Nava, over a painting.

That's your curb appeal.

*Tat to Jewel after she mis-stepped
down from the sidewalk.*

BIRTHDAY

I'm getting too old for my life.

> *Fran Avni, thinking happy, thinking sad.*

He's too young to be old.

> *Jewel, about someone she knows.*

BOTANIST

What do I do with the watermelon crust?

> *Batya, after finishing her meal.*

Feel this. Even the rocks are fresh.

> *Nava, examining a decorative
> stone in a hotel garden.*

BOYS

They consider it a major personal achievement to wear socks for three consecutive days without their mother noticing.

They do not like to waste playtime by going to the bathroom.

They can't wait for their baby teeth to fall out even though they've just grown in.

They don't understand why kids can't drive big-people cars if they promise to be careful.

> *Tova, enumerating the basic factoids about little boys.*

I fell down and hurt my Elmo.

> *Ami, nursing his arm.*

Men don't have nipples. They have muscles.

> *Eitan, pounding his chest and then exclaiming, 'Ouch'.*

Nava pee-ed on my skin, and that's not appropriate.

> *Levi complaining to Naomi*

BUSINESS

Open until closing time.

Gerald, recalling sign in Switzerland.

I have a theory that kids get together once a week for a board meeting. They get out their agendas to schedule when each one is going to have a tantrum, so they don't overlap.

Tova, on why it is that kids never have simultaneous melt-downs.

I wouldn't get a haircut here. There's an axe in the window.

Jewel, looking at a barber shop in a small-town in upstate New York.

-This cookie has 6 grams of fat.

-Is that with tax?

Nava, asking older brother, Eitan, who knows more about accounting.

21

BUSY

We'll have to set you up with some play-dates when I'm studying.

> *Naomi to husband, Jessy, when he was*
> *aimlessly looking for something to do.*

C

CLARITY

For some reason, I've always confused celery with cucumbers.

Ezra, describing his inability
to articulate concepts.

For some reason, I think in Celcius when it's cold and Fahrenheit when it's hot.

Ezra the weatherman.

He's talking baby-Chinese. He wants gum (so do I).

Daveed, explaining the babble of his brother, Ami.

I have a problem: I forget I am old.

Auntie Marlene Kon.

-Who was Confucius?

-He was a philosopher.

-So, he used to research fossils?

Nava, to story-telling Naomi.

CLEAN

I have a laundry in the oven.

Jewel, thinking about the washing machine.

-I have a bump behind my ear.

-Come here, I have medicine.

-No. I don't want you to put spit on my neck.

Batya, avoiding treatment by Tat.

CLOTHING

I love your accessories.

> *Karlie Kloss, pointing to paper stickers*
> *that Ami stuck on Jewel's sweater.*

Ouch! Get rid of it. It's hurting my eyes.

> *Peggi (Cohen), viewing Jewel's*
> *dress as she models it.*

CONSUMER

All I really need is more.

> *Dov, on inconspicuous consumption.*

-I went to Canadian Tire (hardware store).

-Did you get me a generator?

> *Dov asking Jewel about her purchases.*

COOKING

You get an etrog by putting a lemon in the microwave.

Avi Segal, explaining the origins of a citrus fruit.

-The apple juice jar says 'made from concentrate'.
-From concrete?

Mayaan, asking Jewel about nutrition.

CORRESPONDENCE

Dear Mom and Dad, I have some good news and some bad news. The good news is I'm not making up the bad news.

Little Moshe (Segal), writing home from camp.

CREATIVE

Where do we keep the shovels? I want to build a moat in the back yard.

Michi, getting ready for a grand project.

When I was a little girl, I had Barbie dolls with no hair and a Ken doll with one leg.

Naomi, discussing her deprived childhood with Tova.

That was not a cough. It was a comment.

Tat, in denial

It's fictionary.

Talia to Tova, discussing a story.

They said I was a voracious reader.

Jewel, commenting on why the library committee needs her to stay on as a member.

CURE

Ima, I picked this flower for you so you won't be cranky.

> *Yonatan, in the park.*

You'll be his grand-dentist.

> *Naomi, to her childhood dentist upon introducing him to her son, Eitan.*

I'll get the vomitter.

> *Eitan, responding to Naomi's diagnosis of fever.*

-Mum had surgery to put a battery in her
 chest with electric wires that go to her heart.
 (pacemaker)

-So...now Mum's..... a robot?

> *Eitan, reacting to Naomi's news about Jewel.*

-Soon all your baby teeth will fall out and you'll grow
 adult teeth.

-And later all your grown up teeth fall out and you
 get grandma teeth.

-What are grandma teeth?

-Yellow and crooked.

Naomi, discussing
dental development with Nava.

D

DESIRE

I could eat that truck.

> *Jewel, observing a truck painted with*
> *pictures of fruits and vegetables drive by.*

I could fly like a butterfly but I only have toes.

> *Hannah, explaining herself.*

As soon as we get home, let's drive to the forest.

> *Jewel, during a long drive from Toronto.*

DIAGNOSIS

My lips are allergic to my spit.

Mayaan, commenting on her chapped lips.

Yehuda, good thing the doctors told me to wait
three years before conceiving again. Otherwise,
you would have been Naomi.

Jewel, speculating on birth order.

DISASTER

And the people were so bad that G-d sent down a
giant marble on them.

*Noah, after learning in nursery school
about the Biblical Flood [mabul].*

E

EATING

I don't know it by heart. I need my denture.

> *Batya, trying to say Grace after meals*
> *without the text (bencher).*

A vegetarian is a doctor for people who don't eat meat.

> *Avi, with medical insight.*

Years ago when I was young, I was tall and slim. Now I'm tall.

> *Tova, recounting the ravages of age.*

Whenever you go to the supermarket, instead of buying food, you come home with chocolate or cinnamon danish.

> *Jewel, with shopping insight for Lazar.*

-It's supper time. Are you eating supper?

-No, we're eating chips...... I don't know why.

Eitan, uncertain about his pre-dinner food choice.

Can I have a blublely?

*Tehila, asking for a small blue
berry that grows on a bush.*

EDUCATION

We learned three new Hebrew words today – pencil, scissors and book. I don't know how to say them in Hebrew, but those are the words we learned.

Little Moshe (Segal) in kindergarten.

-How are you going to drive a car if you can't even look up a number in the phone book?

-What's a phone book?

Aaron, in a generational disconnect.

A century ago, Andrea would have been a witch.

Csaba, praising his wife's knowledge of the medicinal value of natural foods.

We lost, but we learned much more about the game.

Ami, being philosophical about his soccer game.

I used to be indecisive. Now I don't know what to think.

Dee, tergiversating.

The man who reads the Torah scroll at our synagogue service must have a speech impediment. I can't understand him at all. People say he's very good, but who can tell?

Shoshana Neuer, doing a performance review.

ENVIRONMENT

There is so much glitter everywhere. Why do people leave glitter all over the ground instead of throwing it into a garbage can.

Avi, to his mother, as they walked through the park.

EQUAL

-It's also my birthday today.

-Does that mean we're the same age?

Yonatan, to his father, Noah.

EXERCISE

When I run a lot, I can feel my heart beeping.

Yonatan, listening to himself.

-What were you boys playing downstairs?

-Hitting.

Tova, questioning Michi.

-He started it!

-No! He hit me back first!

Yehuda and Noah, shifting responsibilities.

At Marine Village, I am going to wear my fish-flops.

Hannah, in anticipaticipation.

I think I'll just lie here for a few minutes until my concussion goes away.

Tat, after falling off his bike and banging his head on the pavement.

Mum, you brought very sweaty presents.

Racheli, after running after balloons and balls.

I'll be in the gazebra.

Levi, informing Naomi of his intended
hiding place in the park.

EXCUSE

I don't know why I took your coat. I was already wearing mine.

> *Jake Burak, after mistakenly taking Noah's raincoat.*

You ran the red light. Don't you know how to read colours?

> *Teenagers talking on the street as Tat bikes by.*

EXILE

For the Passover holidays, I'm going back to my homeland.

> *Yonatan, telling his teacher about*
> *Montreal where he was born.*

Who put all those cigarette butts in the wall?

> *Daveed, at the Western Wall in Jerusalem*
> *where people insert small pieces of paper*
> *with their prayers into the cracks.*

EXISTENTIALISM

It's hard to live in a cup.

> *Batya, explaining why her goldfish died.*

F

FATIGUE

I haven't slept for twelve years.

Jewel, reflecting on raising six children.

FEAR

No monsters allowed in this room!

Jewel's sign on kids' room.

The Honk.

*Eitan, talking about the superhero who
turns green and muscular when angry.*

41

FOOD

Grits? That's cream of wheat with dirt in it.

Tat, giving Ezra a culinary insight.

-What are you eating?

-Matza

-I thought matza came in balls.

Naomi, in discussion with her Italian friend during Passover.

It was just lying around.....so you should eat it.

Auntie Marlene, proposing her muffins.

There's only one thing wrong with this cake...there's not enough of it.

Tat, complimenting Genifer on her apple cake.

-What do monkeys like to bake?

-Chocolate chimp cookies.

An original joke by Eitan.

FRIENDS

Never sit next to the girl who brought fish sticks for lunch, after it was in her bag the whole day.

Talia, noting the effect of heat on food.

G

GEOGRAPHY

Mommy: It is so hot today.

Sammy: Why is it hot?

Mommy: Because we live in the Middle East.

Sammy: What? We live in the Middle East?!?

Tova, explaining geography to
Sammy while out walking.

Why don't cities have middle names?

Tat's rhetorical question.

-How was your trip back home?

-Like a long, deep massage on a warm sunny beach.

Noah's description of
the six-hour car ride home with
three energetic kids in the back seat.

GOURMET

Are there any spoiled eggs?

Shua, wondering what's to eat.

GRANDPARENTING

Mazal tov to Jewel and Lazar on the birth of a new grandfather in Dallas.

Synagogue announcer wishing congratulations to welcome Chedva and Ezra's new baby.

-You are very articulate. What 9-year old speaks that way?

-Me!

Maayan, conversing with Tat.

My Grandpa which we call Tata is very tall just like his tall brother. They are kind of like Big Ben and the Empire State Building. His face reminds me of a perfect day to play outside. He has big blue eyes like the sky, a little bit of hair like a few small clouds. He has a short beard like the fresh smelling grass and best of all he has a big bright smile like the big warm sun. Usually when we see him he gives us a nice sweet candy that always makes us happy like we won the World Series. He could be as silly as a clown when he is with us but when he goes to work he can be as serious as a judge. When we have to say goodbye it breaks my heart like broken glass but when he gives us a goodbye hug it feels like a carpet is wrapped around me and that I am hugged by a bear.

Michi about Tat.

You ask if I'm tired? Do you think I look like this for nothing?

Margaret Aster, commenting on all the work she does for her children and grandchildren.

-Do you have any children at home?

-No, our children are your mother and her brothers and sisters.

-I mean little children.

Nava, on family relationships.

-Can you put Vaseline on my lips?

-No, Vaseline is for boys.

Levi, refusing to share
with Jewel for good reason.

H

HAPPY OCCASION

-Mum and Tat are only married forty years??
-Let's see you be married for forty years.

>   *Maayan and Batya planning a party.*

-You're adorable!
-No, I am not Dora!

>   *Exchange between unknown shopper*
>   *and Eitan at the store.*

Good thing I have lips to cover my teeth.

>   *Jewel, reflecting on oral hygiene.*

A bar mitzvah is more important than a wedding.
You only have one bar mitzvah, but you can get
married many times.

>   *Michi, on the realities of life.*

-Where are you going?

-To a wedding.

-Are you marrying Ima? Will she be wearing her
  wedding dress?

> *Ayla, quizzing her father as her
> parents were leaving the house.*

HEALTH

I have a stummy ache.

Levi's self-diagnosis.

For some reason, I have this irresistible urge to roll in the mud and eat garbage.

Dee, regaining consciousness after surgery
to receive a bovine heart valve .

I don't drink apple juice....No! Apple juice makes your teeth lellow.....I drink milk!....milk makes your teeth white!

Three year old Dov, nervously explaining dental
hygiene to his dentist at his first visit.

I feel like a kangaroo. Everyone should have a pouch.

Jewel, enjoying the basket she
affixed to her walker.

HELP

Spiders are your friends.

> *Tat, when asked by Naomi to*
> *get rid of an arachnoid.*

-Just go up to the bullies and fart in their faces.

-But I don't have any more farts left after rest
period.

> *Nava, commenting on her senior*
> *brother's tactical advice.*

HOME

Lessons learned on moving day.

Lesson #1: When the dishwasher delivery guys tell you that they will show up any time from 7 AM to 7 PM, they'll be there at 7 PM.

Lesson#2: don't pack curry powder in a ziplock bag, even if it looks like magical fairy dust when it explodes. Especially if you don't know where the movers put the vacuum.

Naomi, fondly recalling
her move to her new home.

-Is marijuana legal in New York?

-Not in our family.

Batya querying Yehuda.

HOUSE

I was going to ring your bell but you didn't have any front steps.

> *Naomi's neighbour during home renovations.*

-Do you need any furniture for your new apartment?

-I could use a towel.

> *Gadiel Weigensberg, making do with less.*

The only thing my room needs is room.

> *Gadiel Weigensberg,*
> *describing his living quarters.*

Csaba? He's my brother from another mother.

> *Naomi explaining the identity of*
> *a Sarna live-in guest.*

Room service is here!

> *Tova, upon receiving Mommy's tray of food*
> *while in quarantine during the pandemic.*

I

IMPORTANT

I'm President of the Eruv Committee.

> *Moshe, reminding others at Marine*
> *Village of his recent nomination.*

I'm not a hairdresser: I'm really a dentist.

> *Tova's Romanian hairdresser explaining his*
> *professional training while cutting her hair.*

-I finally found my watch.

-Where was it?

-On my wrist. I don't know who put it there.

> *Tat reveling in the discovery .*

IMPOSSIBLE

It's hard to bark and swim at the same time.

Jewel, watching a dog swim in Lake Champlain.

I'm not leaving until I win something.

Someone bemoaning his poor luck at a raffle.

My shadow is so annoying.

*Hannah realizing it doesn't
do what it's supposed to.*

You can't read with your eyes closed.

Jewel, nodding off to dreamland.

INCLUSIVE

All our kids are here.

Tat, not noticing someone was missing.

Is everyone in Montreal called Sarna?

A lecturer from out of town, who coincidentally met or referenced several members of our family within one hour.

INCREDULOUS

-Can we buy a baby for me?

-Babies come out of mommies' tummies.

-Me too? You ate me up?

Little Ernest, figuring out where he came from.

The Earth is a magnet so nothing falls off of it.

Eddie, the astronomer.

-How many nipples does a boy have?

-Five nickels.

Nava, getting a response from Levy.

Is anything wrong? You look happy.

Overheard.

Last night I dreamt in Hebrew. It was great – I spoke without any mistakes at all.

Jewel, very pleased with herself.

Ex-smelly-armpits

Shua declaring the disarming wand charm in Harry Potter (expelliarmus).

J

JUSTICE

Hello Police, I want you to take my mother and father away.

> *Levi on the phone, taking legal recourse after Naomi tossed away his pacifier.*

L

LAWYERS

"Notwithstanding the above provisions..."

-I'm not allowed to stand here?!?

Naomi, reading a legal document to Eitan.

When you die, can I have all your jewelry......
especially the necklace you're wearing.

Nava, staking a claim with Noami.

LIBERAL

My mother was very accepting of people, unless
their sink was dirty.

Bashi, on what parents teach kids.

LINGUISTICS

I spoke with the other children because I know how to speak Hebrew. I just said "Blah, blah blah"........to them.

Talia, at the day care for the first time,
immersed in a new language.

LITERARY

Shakespeare.

-What is a Shakespeare?...Is Shakespeare a type of drink? I think I tasted it once.

Tova, reading bedtime stories.

-Is the bruise on your leg sensitive?

-Yes, to literary criticism.

Lazar, responding to Jewel's concern
after he fell off his bicycle.

LOST AND FOUND

-Ima, where did my treat go?

-In your tummy.

-I want it back now.

Yonatan, mystified by the power of his stomach.

LOVE

-I love you, Mommy.

-I love you too, Nava.

-That's what I also tell my friend, Jakey, after we nap.

Nava, telling Naomi about her true love at school.

-When you come home, I will give you lots and hugs and kisses.

-And hamburgers?

Naomi and Eitan.

I love you, Eitan.

-You can't love me. You're not my mother.

Eitan, discounting his grandmother's affection.

I felt love.

Hannah reacting to baby Evan
waving good-bye to her.

-Tell me about your day, Mamma.

-What do you not know about my day???? We've been together every minute for three weeks straight because of this pandemic. You know when I'm on the phone, what I eat, even when I go to the bathroom.....What could there possibly be about my day that you don't know????

Now go to sleep!

Nava and Naomi at bedtime.

Foods not to eat on the first date: corn on the cob, poppy seed cookies, spaghetti with sauce.

Jewel and Lazar speculating.

M

MARRIAGE

A woman without a husband is a spinster; and a
man without a wife is a splinter.

Batya, taking a wild guess.

You were the best looking person at the cemetery.

Tat to Mum after a funeral.

I can't marry Jakey. He never does what I tell him to do.

Nava, talking about her classmate.

I was hit by another biker, head-on. I went flying
and the bike is all twisted.

-Why didn't you call me right away?

I called all your numbers. No answer.

-I was shopping.

*Lazar, reporting to Jewel on his bike
ride home from the office.*

MONARCHY

She looks pretty good for her age.

> *Sammy, commenting on the Queen*
> *at the Royal Wedding.*

Are the flower maids the children of the bride?

> *Michi, watching a wedding ceremony.*

-Naomi, I found the guest list for your wedding
from ten years ago. Do you want it?

-No, I'm not planning to get married again anytime
soon.

> *Jewel, de-cluttering boxes in the basement.*

MOTHER

I'm available to hold your baby. My arms are bored.

Chedva to Naomi, who was holding baby Nava.

-Did you give your son and daughter-in-law your piano as a house-warming present?

-No. We gave them the house as a house-warming present.

Lila Lowell with Jewel

MOTHER NATURE

The baby is sleeping in your tummy? Do you mean you have a crib in there too?

> *Little Gerald, when Marlene was pregnant.*

MUSIC

You can never have too many trombones.

> *Josh Weigensberg, loaded down with*
> *Marie Josee's band instruments.*

O

OPTIMIST

I don't want to hear any good news, unless it's
about me.

> *Dov, upon being disturbed by an announcement.*

I looked for the book everywhere.

-Did you look elsewhere?

> *Tat, seeking advice*
> *from Dov on a missing volume.*

P

PARENTING

Without a Blackberry? How else can you bill time while rocking kids to sleep?!

Noah, dispensing legal advice at every opportunity.

What's your mother's name?

-Naomi, and her second name is Mamma

Levi, revealing family information.

Hi, Jewel. I called you Jewel.

Levi, mischievously acknowledging he called Mum by her first name.

My mother makes me do puzzles because I'm good at it.

Moshe, explaining his many activities.

-Can we go to a movie?

-Okay.

Can we take another five kids?

-Okay.

-But please don't embarrass me.

> *Michi, worried about Tova's Hebrew*
> *accent and other things.*

Nava, what would you like to do, just me and you?

-Go to Mum's house?

> *Jessy, looking for quality time with Nava.*

I'm going to tell you something that will empower
you: go get it yourself.

> *Yehuda, responding to Daveed who*
> *keeps asking for a glass of water.*

Eddie: Morah Daniella is one more than Abba
because she is 40 and he is 30.

Racheli: No that's 10 more than 30.

Eddie: Actually, she is 44...two fours.

Racheli: So she is 14 years older than Abba... I didn't
realize Morah Daniella was in her 40's.

> *A mathematical dialogue.*

No, Mommy too big....only Avi and only Eddie.

Avi, setting up the singing arrangement.

I'm not bossy. I'm just in charge.

Batya Zobin, explaining authority.

Aw, it's too bad you failed your driver's test.

Jewel and Lazar upon hearing the results from teenager Tova.

Where are you going?

-Out

I have an important question.

-What is it? I have to go.

How was your day?

Nava, trying to hold on to Mama

PARSIMONIOUS

When I buy a convertible car, I won't have to pay so much because it doesn't have a roof.

> *Sammy, contemplating a wise purchase.*

PHILOSOPHY

-The font of ideas...

-You mean, fount?

-The Times Roman of ideas...

> *Yehuda, during a discourse at the table.*

Now that will stay there forever.

> *Nava, after urinating in the snow.*

Why did the man eat bread?

Because he had water in his ear.

> *Earliest recorded original riddle by Shirley Sarna.*

PICNIC

Pick up the onion under the picnic table. We wouldn't want the skunk to have bad breath.

Jewel, worrying about animal welfare.

PRAYER

Are you allowed to spell on the Sabbath?

Helen Liberman's legal question.

PRECAUTION

If I'm not careful, I might get Athlete's Face.

Jewel, massaging Sammy's feet
after being cautioned by Tova.

I don't like leaving a gift for someone who makes
more money than I do.

Asher Neudorfer contemplating leaving
a Christmas tip for the postman.

PRECISION

I didn't hit her. I, um, clapped her, on the head.

> *Yonatan, when asked why Hannah, who was sitting next to him eating lunch, was crying.*

-Don't go in. They're having a private conversation.

-I won't disturb them: I just want to hear what they're saying.

> *Eitan, clarifying his intent to Naomi.*

Why is that man holding a paint brush to the Torah?

> *Hannah asking about the pointer.*

Someone who is zealous is a zealot. Is someone who is jealous, a jeolot?

> *Shira Browns, visiting with her family.*

PRIDE

Even if I were a piece of garbage, I wouldn't want to be thrown in the garbage.

> *Mayaan, lamenting over the discarding of a stale, store-bought chocolate cake.*

-I've been wearing this shirt for four days.

-You know, when your cousin, Asa, was fighting in the war this summer, he didn't change his socks or underwear for two weeks.

-Wow, he's so lucky! My mother would never let me do that.

> *Nine year old Michi and Jewel on the realities of dressing.*

PROFILING

Walterstein

> *Jessy, uttering what he thinks is a*
> *typical Ashkenazi family name.*

Do you know Herb? You look exactly like Herb.

I mean, you wear the same shirt.

> *Mentioned to Tat at a breakfast.*

PUNCTUALITY

The class party will end approximately at 6 or 6:15
pm. Please pick up your child exactly on time.

> *Note from Michi's teacher.*

R

REALITY

She has the right to bare arms.

> *Jewel, looking at photos of Batya*
> *wearing short sleeved tops.*

-How many kids are in your class?

-All of them.

> *Yonatan, responding to Mum.*

-Why don't you sit down and read a book?

-My body won't allow me.

> *Yonatan, actively discussing his*
> *physiology with Jewel.*

RELIGION

You have to take a bath so that you will be clean.

-For Passover?

Nava, asking a relevant question.

This is the church Tat doesn't go to...and this is the other church he doesn't go to.

Jewel explaining a photo of Tat on his bike between two church spires.

Let me tell you how I went from being a camp counselor to Chief Rabbi of the United Arab Emirates.

Yehuda, addressing summer camp alumni.

S

SAD

Now he's saying kat-dish.

*Gerald, on hearing about someone
mourning his deceased feline.*

SARCASM

That's like putting lingerie on a monkey.

*Dee, commenting on his friend's plan to renovate
his house located in a bad neighbourhood.*

SCIENCE

How do they make recycled paint? Do they peel it off the walls?

Jewel, asking a hardware question.

Abba, does everyone know that you have a lot of hair on your body? Should I tell them?

Avi, making physiological discovery.

SECRET

Naomi: ....Now enter your password.

Mummy: Password?...my password?!? (blank stare).

Naomi: Ya, password. Yours.

Mummy: I don't know....what is it?

Naomi: I'm not telling you.

Mummy: Why not? It's my password!

Naomi, helping Mum log on to Facebook.

SENSITIVE

I am a sweat-detector.

> *Moshe, after sitting on the shoulders*
> *of a student dancing and hopping.*

I will pray for you.

> *Eitan to Ami, after he accidentally*
> *broke the light fixture in the basement*
> *where they were throwing balls.*

SIGHT

Don't worry. I have X-ray vision. I saw through the bus.

> *Tova, anticipating a pedestrian darting out from*
> *behind another vehicle as she was driving.*

SPACE

I don't want to be here. I don't want to be there. I
don't want to be anywhere.

Dee, finding no place for himself.

SPEAKING

Whenever I want to say hospital, for some reason I
say airport.

Chedva, according to Ezra.

It is not nice to talk Russian hora.

Yonatan, explaining the rules of slander.

SPIES

Undercovered.

> *Moshe, describing a secret world.*

SPORTS

First, let me see you run.

> *Dee to Jewel, in her 9th month of pregnancy when she invited him to play tennis with her.*

I'm afraid I'm going to drain.

> *Eddie to Chedva, on why he doesn't want to go swimming.*

Consider it sports equipment.

>*Tova, consoling Jewel over having*
>*to temporarily use a walker.*

SUMMER

What are you doing?

-Nothing.

>*Michi, methodically pounding the sand on*
>*the beach with a rock in a minnow net.*

SUMMERTIME

I like Marine Livage.

>*Daveed, in the country by the lake.*

SUPERPHARM

Where are all the animals?

> *Michi, looking around the drugstore.*

SURPRISE

Maayan, brace yourself!

> *Batya to Maayan, when Tova was about to give
> her a present of new clothes. This was after
> Tova gave Moshe turquoise socks with glitter.*

Why did I wake up covered in smiley-face stickers
this morning?

> *Tova, after Ilan decorated her
> pajamas while she slept.*

-I wanted to see if my underwear came alive in the dark.

-Ezra, explaining why he slowly closed the bureau drawer on his lower lip.

> *Wake me up when my birthday*
> *surprise gets here.*

Tat, on preparing for the surprise that wasn't.

-Nothing in that washroom works.

-Maybe it's an exhibit.

> *Tova, explaining the Museum to Tat.*

T

TASTE

My favourite food is...ice!

Michi, the gourmet.

One part of my brain is wondering why I don't open my chips. A second part is saying it's because I am not finished my drink. A third part is wondering if I should eat them at the same time.

Racheli, in a quandry.

TASTIER

My favourite vegetable is cow.

Noah, considering the food options.

TASTIEST

Could you ask mommy and daddy if they could also buy me a cloud?

> *Ilan to Talia at the park, when he saw*
> *a boy eating cotton candy.*

THIRSTY

-What are you putting in your coffee?

-Amaretto. I use it instead of sugar. Mmm. It needs more sugar.

> *Jewel, tasting her drink.*

This baby has surplus spit.

> *Batya, holding a young sibling*

TIME

When were you born?

-1950

Is that in the 80's?

Moshe, cross-examining Jewel on her birthday.

When it's night, every hour is dark o'clock

Tat, commenting on winter.

In the olden times, you would have to send a text in an envelope.

Eitan, thinking back.

TIMING

It looks like Mommy started a very, very important phone call. I better whine and take a fit.

Ilan thinking, as Tova takes the call

It doesn't matter if I help Mum. She's going to win anyway.

Daveed, the card master

TIRED

You're asleep.

-No, I'm listening.

Jewel, in denial

TRUST

Give me all your money. I'll invest it for you.

Moshe, age 11, advising Daveed, age 8.

U

ULTIMATUM

Unless you get into the car right now, you'll
have to stay with Mum and go to a funeral and a
gynecologist appointment with her.

Tova, presenting choices to Sammy.

UNDERSTAND

I'm trying to make magic, but it's not working.

*Ilan, after trying to make a small toy
disappear under a napkin and repeating
abracadabra several times.*

Who created Starbucks?

Racheli contemplating.

I know Swedish from reading the IKEA furniture
catalogue.

*Aaron Koller telling
Tat about his new vocabulary.*

W

WANT

You're not really hungry: you're thirsty.

> *Tat, to kids asking for ice cream.*

You're not really thirsty: you're tired.

> *Jewel, to kids asking for a drink at bedtime.*

WARNING

-Mommy, there's a fly in the car.

-Does it have its seat-belt on?

> *Sammy and Tova having a driving discussion.*

The arctic is cold because it's cold in outer space.

> *Shua, the weatherman.*

WEDDINGS

We'll be wearing our best software.

Tat, lamenting non-attendance at
Talia's wedding, except by Zoom.

WIT

"I've always felt concerned about my need to give advice," one attendee said. "The first meeting was great, though if you ask me, they should have done it a little differently."

Yehuda, from his article on
compulsive givers of advice.

WORK

-You should get a job fixing bicycles.

-Where would I get one?

-You could be our personal bicycle fixer.

> *Neighbour's eight-year old, as*
> *Tat repaired her flat tire.*

When I grow up, I'm going to buy a saw.

> *Eitan, watching Tat cut wood in the back yard.*

I want to cut down the bushes. Can I have the
tweezers?

> *Eitan, the gardener.*

Y

YEP

The best way to get rid of a bee is to spray starch it.

Ezra, continuing a family tradition.

YOUNG

-Is that a new baby?

-Yes, it's still under warranty.

Jessy, commenting on a new family member.

YOUNGER

There was an old lady like you..... but you're not old.

Batya, telling Jewel an engrossing story.

PART TWO:
REAL WORDS ON THEIR OWN

Children are notorious users of words. Their grasp of the word is often as tenuous as a grasp of a wet and wiggling fish.

We have collected words for this dictionary which best typify the ability of children to confidently or seriously or light-heartedly speak in a language that has been thrust upon them.

Let us remember though, that language is only one of several means of expression: a child would prefer to scream, kick or smile if his or her needs would more readily be satisfied. The very use of the listed words indicates the child's preference for language as a means of communication. The malformation or contortion which the word suffers indicates the incomplete grasp, or in another sense, the excessive expectation the child brings to the force and effect of diction.

We have chosen words which, although twisted in meaning, do for the most part have a true existence and significance in the English language. As may be noted, a few are cunning, many disarming, all innocent.

A

ABORT

on deck, as in "all abort".
The train conductor calls "All
Aboard."

ACE OF SPACE

a playing card. A powerful
one to have in any card
game.

AIR COMMISSIONER

air cooling device. A very
valuable machine to have in
hot weather.

AIR PAIN

an air vehicle. How does
an airplane that weighs so
much fly through the air?

AISLE

a river in Egypt. A natural
source of irrigation and
hydro power.

ALL WHITE

all is right. A pre-condition
to being happy is to
recognize everything is in
its best place.

AMMONIA

a medical condition. Pneumonia is a dreaded disease that usually requires a trip to the hospital.

AND

a black insect; also, the end of an arm. The industrious ant teaches us many things, even if it does not have a hand.

ARROW

sixty minutes. A watch only shows one hour at a time.

ASH

trash. Trash becomes garbage when it is not usable.

B

BANK IT   a warm cover. A blanket not only warms, it comforts.

BEARD   an adult beverage. Beer is not a drink for children.

BEREAVE   breathe. We have to open our mouths and noses to take in air.

BIRD   a spontaneous expulsion of gas from the mouth. You can't help making this noise to clear your stomach.

BLASTER   white powder used to cover wall cracks. Somehow, the plaster sticks to the wall in a flat way.

BREAST   air inhaled, as in "a breast of fresh air". The reason for breathing.

BROWN   to die in water. There is no colour in drowning, only sorrow.

BURT   a flying fowl. How do birds rise up and come down so gracefully?

C

CAD   a feline. Many people think cats are lazy but smart.

CAKE   a mantle worn by a mythical hero. A cape does not have any. pockets: so, what good does it do?

CAMEL BREAD   bread with kimmel seeds. Many people like it toasted in a sandwich.

CAPE   a dessert made of flour, often with icing. The problem is that the icing is usually better than the cake it covers.

CEMENT   lower floor of a house. Downstairs can be cold, damp, dark, spooky, but always quiet.

CHEQUE MAID   a chess move. The only way to win the game: by taking the king.

CHEW — clothing for the foot. It is important that shoes match and are worn on the appropriate feet.

CHICKEN — a room used for food preparation. Sometimes, the whole family hangs out in the kitchen.

CHIT MONK — squirrel's relative. The chipmunk is smaller and cuter than its larger cousin.

CHOP SEWER — a Chinese food. Some people don't like such a salty dish.

CHOPPING — searching through stores for purchases. Sometimes it can take hours if you don't know what you are looking for.

D

DART

black. The night is always black
outside, but hopefully not inside.

DENTAL FLUFF

a string used to clean between
teeth. A toothbrush is not
enough.

DIPPER

a mechanical device used for
zipping. The inventor of this item
is a hero, except when it breaks.

DUMMY

where food goes. It probably
looks like a big plastic bag.

DRAIN

a body organ used for thinking.
Some people have big ones,
making them smarter.

E

EAST   leavening agent. What a magical
way to make bread.

F

FATS OF LIFE   reality. What is true is what is
                      real, most of the time.

FERSTER   a university teacher. This is
                      an occupation many aspire
                      to, because of the respect
                      students give.

FING   an object. What is tangible
                      could also be intangible.

FIRSTY   a sensation requiring the
                      drinking of liquid. It does not
                      matter what you drink, as long
                      as it contains lots of water.

FLUTE   a viral infection causing fever.
                      Being sick is no fun, even with
                      all the attention you get.

G

GLUBS   hand warmers. Certain people love mittens while others favour fingered gloves.

GRAPES   mechanical device for slowing cars, as in "step on the grapes!" It is not good practice to drive with one foot on the gas and the other on the brake.

GRILL   a young female. There is no male equivalent.

GROW   a black bird. They can be very scary when they land in flocks and make their caw-ing noise.

H

HAND CUPS police restraining device. It is next to impossible to get out of hand-cuffs or do anything with your arms.

HARD an organ in the chest. It beats like a drum, always with the same rhythm.

HEARSE four legged animal. A horse is a strong and faithful animal because it never complains.

HOLD a perforation. The wonderful thing about a hole is that both sides of it are the same.

HOT to jump on one foot. We actually move faster by hopping like a kangaroo.

HUM BREE a feeling only food can satisfy. There are favourite foods, and then items that just fill up a stomach without much taste.

I

IMPARTMENT   important. Important is not
                    necessarily like urgent: more
                    like first things first.

I RAN   A metal. It's strange that
                    some foods contain iron, and
                    that it is healthy to eat.

J

JELLY   happy ("for he's a jelly good
fellow"). Being happy makes
others happy as well.

K

KOOL

a place populated by students. Teachers take the place of parents for most of the day.

KOVERED

cupboard. The only place to safely store fragile dishes.

KRACK

sound made by a duck. It's strange that every sound for every occasion is a quack.

L

LIE BERRY

a place of books. No talking, no food, no wrestling, just reading.

LOST IN FOUNTAIN

where lost clothes and articles are kept. You get some of the best stuff in the Lost and Found.

M

MARVEL   a round glass ball. The more marbles, the more they look like a cache of diamonds.

MAT   angry. Losing control is another excuse for being mad.

MIKER WAVE   an oven. What a magic box it is that warms things up but doesn't get hot.

MOP   a flying insect. Moths used to eat clothes and make holes. That stopped once moth balls were invented, and polyester took over from wool.

MOP OILY   a board game. Even small children now understand the economics of monopoly.

MR. FISH   troublesome. Both kids and adults share this trait.

MUST STAFF   growth of hair on the upper lip. Some men like to wax it, curl it or simply shave it off.

N

NAPPLE

a popular fruit. You can make sauce or apple cake with it.

NEOPLOLITICS

three-flavoured ice cream with layers of chocolate, vanilla and strawberry.

NO

white frozen rain. Snow can be fluffy or ice.

O

OFFER

a person who writes books.
Authors like to hear from
their readers.

OVERFLOATING

when water goes over the
edge as in "The toilet is
overfloating!" What a wonder
this is, especially when it
drowns the floor.

P

PAINED   oil-based or latex colouring liquid. Everything looks new when it is freshly painted.

PEAS   please. A polite introduction to a request.

PETARD   a six or twelve-stringed musical instrument. Many folk singers entertain using a guitar in an emotional way.

PIG   a dried sweet fruit. The difference between a dried and fresh fig is astounding.

POLO BEAR   a white arctic animal. What a majestic animal, covered in an all-white coat.

POND   chess piece. The pawn is an expendable member of the team but not really.

POSED   a short pillar often supporting
                         a fence. Good fences and posts
                         make good neighbours.

POST CARD   marine police patrol. They go up
                         and down the coast looking to
                         help stranded boaters.

R

RAISIN — a black bird. It's hard to tell the difference between a crow and a raven.

REEL — a round rubber object rotating on an axle. A reel is a reel.

RIGHT — a state of maturity of fruit. Fruit can be very delicate, soft, hard, juicy or wrinkled.

ROAST CAKE — a skate with wheels. Roller derbies are the best places to use these these.

RUDE — subterranean part of a tree. Most roots dive very deeply into the ground.

S

SCREAM — used in movie projection. The anticipation of seeing the show on the screen is always tremendous.

SEA-BELL — a safety restraining device in a car. It may be uncomfortable, but the seat-belt is the best protection in the event of a sudden stop.

SEEP — to lie dormant. Sleeping and dreaming go together. Nightmares disturb sleep.

SHARK — reaction to an electric current. Never stick anything into the electric outlet, especially metal, or you might get a shock.

SHAVE — sunless spot (the shave of a tree). The temperature is cooler in the shadow of tree leaves.

SHEEP — a linen mattress covering. We change our sheets every so often.

SICK CAR   a tobacco product. The smelliest
            smoke comes from the cigar.

SINGING   radio speakers in a car.
HEATERS   Sometimes the amplifiers don't
            work well enough.

SIP   a crunchy potato snack, Usually
            too salty or oily and goes with
            any meal.

SMOKES MEAT a delicatessen meat. It is best
            in a sandwich with pickles and
            mustard.

SNIPPERS   casual shoes. Never walk bare-foot
            in the house.

STY   the heavens. The sky is home to
            the sun, clouds and stars.

SUPPER AID spread apart. Either we are
            together or separate.

T

TAMBOURINE   orange citrus fruit. The tangerine is the smaller sister of the orange and the grapefruit.

THUMB TAG   tack for pressing with the thumb. The better fastener is magnetic.

TIE YARD   fatigued. Whether you exercise or sit still, you can always feel tired.

TOILET TREES   cosmetics and stuff. Perfumes and creams make the day.

TOMATO SOCKS   substance poured on spaghetti. It is hard to make a good first impression by eating this dish, even though it is delicious.

TOOTH TAPE   tooth cleaner. Brushing is always a chore, but an essential one for healthy teeth.

TUFFS

tusks. Elephants use their tusks to fight and to protect.

TURBAN TIME

a paint solvent. It may smell strong, but turpentine does the job.

U

UNDER A WRIST — taken into custody by police officer - "You're under arrest."

UNIFIER — humidifier. Breathing is much easier in a slightly humid environment.

UNIVERSE — female reproductive organ. Babies are not born from the stomach.

URF — the contents of ground. There is a difference between earth and dirt.

V

VARVA-QUE   outdoor roasting apparatus. Barbacue is mostly ash and fire.

VIRUS   a flower. The elegance and scent of the iris is unbeatable.

W

WALNUT   book shelves in a unit. A bookcase filled with reading material warms a room.

WANE   precipitation. People usually can't find their umbrellas when they need them.

WELT   a pit in the ground with water at the bottom. Make sure the bucket doesn't have a hole.

WHIFF   a preposition denoting accompaniment. Being with is usually better than being without.

WINK   flying limb of a bird. This is why we can't fly using our arms.

WOES   a prized flower. Red roses are a favorite, even if they don't have a perfume about them.

WOOL   the planet. The world is either round or oval.

Y

YEARS	auditory organs in the head. Usually they hear; often, not.
YEH-WHOA	a light colour. Yellow is a cousin of green, red and orange.

YEST (LAST) BUT NOT LEAST

I'm not procrastinating. I'm delegating to my future self.

Maayan's rationale.

Grabbing is what I do best.

Eitan responding to Jewel reproach
not to grab Nava's book

The boundary between heaven and earth is more permeable than the border between the USA and Canada.

Yehuda recalling his confrontation at the border
during the pandemic, after Jewel told him about
a dream visit from her late grandmother.

Why are you wearing a Mormon dress?

>*Jewel, still 'loopey' after surgery, reacting to Naomi's long spring green dress.*

Stop pulling on my under-arms. You'll make me have flabby upper arms.

>*Jewel, reacting to Lazar's attempt at massage*

There are more words in Yiddish than ververkeh (squirrel).

>*Yehuda the grammarian.*

It's time to do your exercises.

-I'm making the fruit salad

You're procrastinating.

-I have nothing to do but procrastinate.

>*Jewel responding to Tova's urging to exercise post-surgery.*

I get my vaccine at 1:30pm. If I die, please know there is no way I could ever repay you for the affection and care you have lavished on me, and I hereby leave you all my DvDs.

>*Michelle Franklin's last will and testament.*

I have not asked you this in fifteen years. Can I
borrow the car?

Naomi making a request to her father.

Restaurant food not to order on the first date:

Spaghetti, corn on the cob, poppy seed hamen-
tashen.

Jewel making a menu.

Ask my grandfather what time it is, and he'll first
tell you how the watch is made.

Bashi's family.

My head is like a gragger (Purim noise maker).

Bashi's self impression.

Where there's a whistle, there's a train.

*Bashi teaching nursing students
about bodily expression.*

Did you wash your hands?

Yes.

Did you brush your teeth?

I will take that request in two minutes.

Eitan responding strategically to his mother.

Why is your room so messy?

-It's complicated.

Nava explaining to her mother

My grandmother was born in Rwanda.

*A friend's grandchild in grade school
talking about Rouyn Noranda, Quebec,
during a discussion of Rwanda, Africa.*

The best place to shop is at your parents' house

Naomi, leaving with great bargains

Who are all these people?

Noah suddenly surrounded by all his childre

A handicap walker: Consider it sports equipment.

*Tova in response to Jewel's dismay
at having to use a walker to get around.*

You fell off your bike today?

-Yes, and I have a yeast infection.

That must have been some fall!

Naomi listening to
Jewel describing her bruises

THE OFFERS (AUTHORS)

Who exactly are the creative minds behind this major contribution to the world of dictionaries?

Chedva, Ezra, Dov, Jessy, Naomi, Jewel, Lazar, Noah, Josa, Tova, Gerald, Yehuda, Michelle

Sammy, Ilan, Talia, Michi

(back) Yisrael, Racheli, (front) Tehilla, Yehoshua, Avi

Yonatan, Ariel, Hannah, Ayla

Levi, Eitan, Nava

(back) Batya, Moshe, Maayan,
(front) Daveed, Hillel, Ami.

USA — Michelle (Waldman) Sarna and Yehuda Sarna, Batya, Maayan, Moshe, Daveed, Amital, Hillel/ New York

Chedva (Deutsch) Sarna and Ezra Sarna, Racheli, Yisrael, Avi, Yehoshua, Tehilla/ Houston

Canada — Jewel (Weigensberg) Sarna and Lazar Sarna/ Montreal

Israel Dov (Dee) Sarna/ Montreal

Naomi Sarna and Jessy Benbaruk Eitan, Nava, Levi/Montreal

Josa (Alley) Sarna and Noah Sarna Yonatan, Hannah, Ayla, Ariel/Toronto

Israel — Tova (Sarna) Segal and Gerald Segal

Talia (and Michael Saar), Sammy, Michi, Ilan/ Modi'in

And — Thanks to all the other named and unnamed contributors.

ABOUT THE EDITOR

LAZAR SARNA currently writes and lectures on literary and professional issues, and practices law in Montreal Canada. He is the author of the poetry collections *He Claims He is the Heir* and *Letters of State*, both through Porcupine's Quill, as well as the novels *The Man Who Lived Near Nelligan*, Coach House Press and *Book Bin Baby*, Adelaide Books. His poetry has appeared in *Antigonish Review, Canadian Forum, Canadian Literature, Descant, Fiddlehead,* and *Prism International*. The poetry book *He Claims He is the Heir* was nominated as finalist for the Quebec Writers Federation Award.

Sarna has lectured at the McGill University Law Faculty, and the John Molson School of Business at Concordia University. As a member of the Quebec Bar Association, he has addressed professional credit conferences and pleaded before most court jurisdictions including the Supreme Court of Canada. His numerous legal publications are frequently cited by the courts in Canada.

Made in the USA
Monee, IL
27 February 2022

91978830R00083